What on Earth?
Life in the
Grasslands

What on Earth?

What are these

beetles pushing?
Turn this page for the answer.

First published in 2005 by
Book House an imprint of
The Salariya Book Company
25 Marlborough Place
Brighton
BN1 1UB

HB ISBN 1-905087-45-4
PB ISBN 1-905087-46-2

Visit our website at **www.book-house.co.uk**
for free electronic versions of:
You Wouldn't Want to be an Egyptian Mummy!
You Wouldn't Want to be a Roman Gladiator!
Avoid joining Shackleton's Polar Expedition!
Avoid Sailing on a 19th Century Whaling Ship!

Due to the changing nature of internet links, The Salariya Book Company
has developed an online list of websites related to the subject of this book.
This site is updated regularly. Please use this link to access the list:
http://www.book-house.co.uk/WOE/grasslands

A catalogue record for this book is available from the British Library.

Printed and bound in China.

Editor: Ronald Coleman
Senior Art Editor: Carolyn Franklin
DTP Designer: Mark Williams

Picture Credits Dave Antram: 23(b), Julian Baker: 8, 9(t),
12, 13(b), Elizabeth Branch: 1, 2, 3, 4, 5, 8(b), 14, 15, 22,
Fiammetta Dogi: 6, 7, John Shaw, NHPA: 16, Kevin Schafer,
Corbis: 20, David Samuel Robbins, Corbis: 24,
George E. Marsh Album, NOAA: 25, Mary Clay/Dembinsky
Photo Associates: 29, Corbis: 23(t), Digital Vision: 10, 11,
13, 18, 19, 21, 26, 27, Digital Stock: 16, 17, PhotoDisc: 28,
John Foxx: 30, 31

What on Earth?

DUNg!

The dung beetle (tumblebug)
lives off animal droppings and
decaying plants. It makes balls of
droppings bigger than itself. The
beetles then roll each ball into a
hole. The female lays an egg on
top of it and covers it up.

niffy pongs!

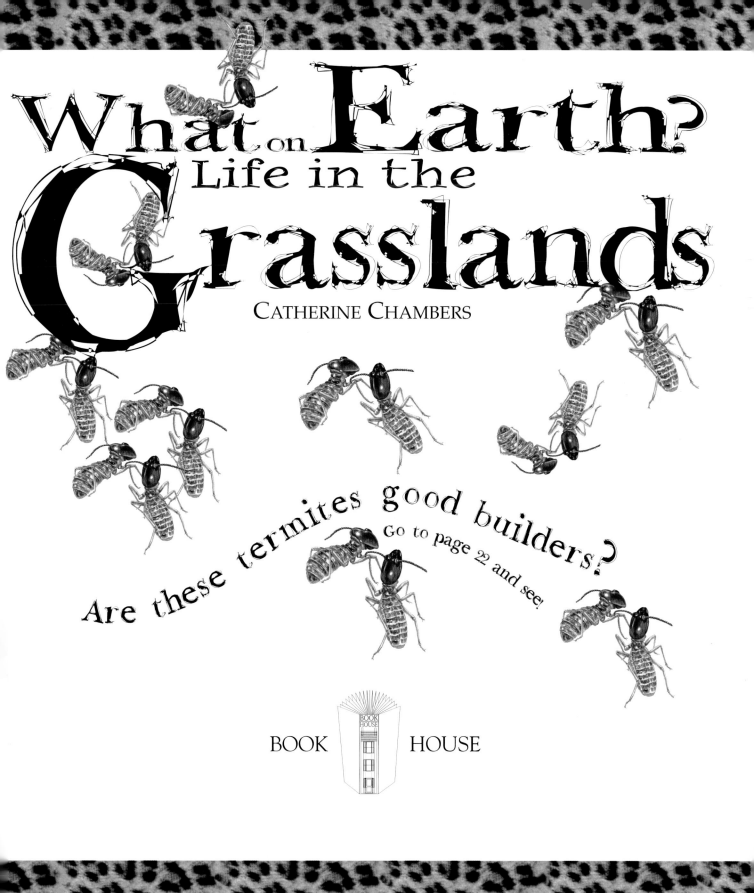

What on Earth? Life in the Grasslands

CATHERINE CHAMBERS

Are these termites good builders?
Go to page 22 and see!

BOOK HOUSE

Contents

What on Earth?

Yum...yum!

Termite soldier

Nasty habits!

Some termites keep live beetles in their mounds. They drain the liquid and feed on it.

Introduction

Grasslands are vast areas of grasses that cover huge areas of land. They are formed naturally but some are created through forest clearance, animal herding and farming. Grasslands may be flat or hilly and grasses can be short, or tall and feathery.

Are all grasslands the same?

There are two main grassland zones. Hot tropical grasslands are hot and dry with one or two rainy seasons. They may be dotted with small trees or bushes. Dry temperate grasslands are very hot and dry but very cold in the winter.

Is all grass the same?

Grasses are affected by climate and habitat. Some grasses only grow to about ankle height while others can grow to about three metres (10 feet) tall. A blade of grass can be very thin or as wide as a broom handle.

What's happening underground?

Go to page 14.

Grasslands

Vast open areas of grassland are home to many animals. This scene shows many plant and animal species in a hot tropical grassland in East Africa. Dry temperate grasslands look brown and parched in the summer and are often blackened by fires. Snow can fall in winter.

Weaver bird

Vulture

Wildebeest

Termite mound

Impala

Cheetah

African striped skink

Marabou stork

Dung beetle

Cape buffalo

Leopard

Elephant

Giraffe

Zebra

Springbok

Kudu

Marabou stork

7

Where are grasslands?

Hot tropical grasslands spread out over the hottest part of the world. They stretch across Africa, South America, southern Asia and Australia. They often lie between forests and deserts. Most temperate grasslands stretch through parts of Europe, Asia and the Americas.

Canada

North America

Atlantic Ocean

Pacific Ocean

South America

Antarctica

Areas of grassland shown on maps.

Rhino and zebra in the park!

Rhino

Zebra

Rhino and zebra flourish on the grasslands of eastern and southern Africa. Some grasslands have become protected national parks.

Europe
Asia
Africa
Pacific Ocean
Indian Ocean
Australia
Antarctica

In Africa, grasslands spread over about half of the continent.

In Asia there are grasslands on high plateaux between huge mountain ranges where it is too cold and dry for many trees to grow.

America's Great Plains (grasslands) lie next to the Rocky Mountains in what is called 'rain shadow land', (land that is dry because the mountains shelter it from rain).

What are grasslands called?

What on Earth?

What's in a name?

'Savannah' is a Native American word for grasslands.

Grasslands grow on every continent except Antarctica at the South Pole. In Africa and South America, grasslands are called 'savannah'. In North America they are called 'prairies'. The Russian word for grasslands is 'steppes' and in South America tall swaying grasslands are called 'pampas'.

9

Are grasslands hot or cold?

Hot tropical grasslands are hot all year round. Temperate grasslands bake in hot summers but are bitterly cold in the winter. High in the central Asian grasslands, summers are short and fiercely hot but winters are long and freezing. Grasses here are short and ground-hugging to survive the blasts of icy wind.

Elephants

The African elephant is now only found in the grasslands of east and central Africa. The elephant is considered an endangered species.

Are grasslands wet or dry?

Grasslands thrive in areas that are too dry for forests to grow but have more rainfall than deserts. Some hot tropical grasslands have about three very wet months a year. But others have up to eight months of rainfall, enough for some trees to grow as well as grass.

Is the weather wild?

Yes. Fierce thunderstorms, hailstones, high winds and tornadoes can rage across the grasslands. Tornadoes often occur in the North American prairies. Lightning sometimes sets fire to dry grasslands.

What on Earth?

Big muscles!

An elephant's trunk has 40,000 muscles which give it great strength and movement.

An elephant uses its trunk like an arm. The tip of its trunk is sensitive enough to pick up a pin.

How does grass grow?

Grass root systems can spread outwards and **downwards**! Waxy stems which grow up from the roots, sprout leaves. As the plant grows it makes a spikelet with lots of flowers. Seeds form in the spikes at the base of the flowers. Some grasses sprout fresh leaves from **scattered** seeds, while others grow from buds just under the soil's surface.

A grass seed spike is like a feathery arrowhead. This helps it to float on the wind. It has a sharp tail to anchor it firmly in the soil when it lands. This is how seeds spread.

Can grass cope with grazers?

Grazing animals crop tufts of grass very close to the ground. Grass grows again very quickly.

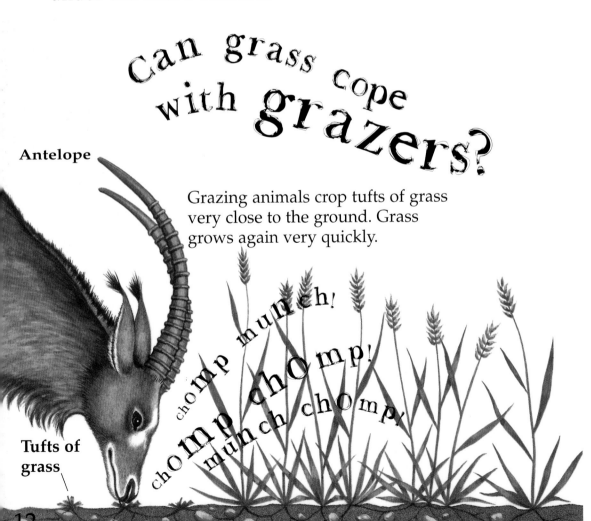

Antelope

chomp munch!

chomp chomp!

munch chomp!

Tufts of grass

What on Earth? Disaster?

Fierce fires turn grasslands into ashes. But after a fire, grass plants are triggered into producing new shoots. Fire can actually **renew** grasslands!

sizzle!

sizzle!

sizzle!

African buffalo herd - Okavango Delta, Botswana, Africa.

What's underground?

Only a third of the grass plant grows above ground, the rest of it forms a tangle of roots and runners in the soil. Tiny hairs on the grass roots absorb the minerals and water it needs from the soil. Grassland soils vary. Tropical grasses grow in dry, shallow soil. Temperate grasses grow in deep, rich, dark soil. A teeming mass of wildlife share the grassland soil.

The burrowing owl (below right) eats small mammals and large insects. It often lays its eggs in other creatures' empty nests.

Prairie dog family

Grass

Roots

Prairie dog

What on Earth?

Too small to see?

Protozoa

Algae

Bacteria

Fungus

Virus

Tiny bacteria and protozoa which are too small to see, help to break down dead matter. Algae and fungus help to feed the soil.

These insects eat smaller insects that can cause plant disease. They also clear up dead plant matter.

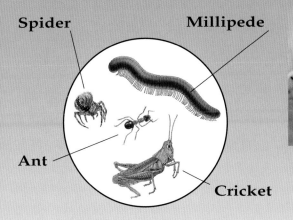

Spider

Millipede

Ant

Cricket

No it's a North American prairie dog, a member of the rat family. Like rats, its teeth keep growing because it wears them down with constant chewing. Prairie dogs live in packs and build huge networks of underground burrows called towns.

The rattlesnake lives in a burrow. It eats small mammals and birds and eats other snakes too. Some species of rattlesnake lay eggs, others give birth to live snakes.

Burrowing owl

Coyote

Rattlesnake

A black-footed ferret kills a prairie dog and then takes over its home

Slug

Worm

15

Do other plants grow in grasslands?

Grassland is full of wildflowers and is scattered with shrubs or trees. These plants have to survive in difficult conditions. Flowers in temperate grasslands must cope with freezing weather. They grow low to the ground to shelter from biting winds. Their leaves are tightly curled to keep in warmth.

Spring on the Texas prairie (left). Wildflowers bloom everywhere. This temperate grassland brims with bee-loving flowers like clover. Some flowers like broom snakeweed and rayless goldenrod are very poisonous.

Where is the great serengeti?

The great Serengeti grasslands meet the forested foothills of Mount Kilimanjaro in Tanzania (below). Here, thorny shrubs grow, and acacia trees spread their canopies of broad, leafy branches. Lace-like acacia leaves close up tightly to keep in moisture.

What on Earth?

What's so special about the baobab tree?

In drier parts of the grasslands the great baobab tree dots the landscape. Its huge hollow trunk holds water and every part of the tree can be used by humans.

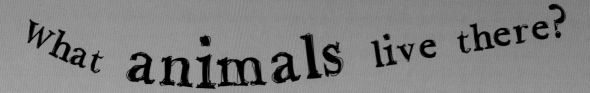

What animals live there?

Great herds of large herbivores (plant-eating mammals) have roamed grasslands for millions of years. They have strong hooves for galloping across hard ground. Their teeth and stomachs can chew and digest stiff grasses. Bison and cattle have **four** stomachs!

Which animal is a nibbler?

Spiky seeds

Some grasses have smooth seeds which are eaten and scattered along with an animals' droppings. Other plants have spiky seeds which spread because they land on animals' fur.

Zebra

Giraffe

Zebra and giraffes drink from a water hole. Giraffes are browsers. They nibble leaves from trees and tall shrubs.

Why do **leopards** have spots?

A leopard's spots help to hide, or camouflage it amongst grasses.

What are predators?

A leopard is a predator, a creature that hunts other animals for food. Leopards and other big cats are attracted by huge herds of herbivores that graze the grassland. Predators stalk weak, old or very young animals or those that have strayed from the herd.

What on Earth?

Ants beware!

The giant anteater has no teeth. But its sticky tongue can slurp up

30,000 ants
each day!

Do birds live in grasslands?

Grasslands are perfect habitats for lots of bird species from **huge** Australian emus to tiny Hungarian larks. Smaller birds eat grass seeds, berries, insects and grubs. Larger birds such as emus, ostriches and rheas chew leaves and roots as well as eating seeds and berries. They also eat small lizards, birds and snakes. Birds are good for the grassland. They spread seeds which are shed in their droppings and also eat insects and pests.

Greater rhea

The greater rhea lives on the South American pampas.

Speedy rhea!

Like ostriches, the rhea cannot fly but it runs at 64 kilometres (40 miles) per hour!

Long tall rhea

What do vultures eat?

Not all birds are seed and insect eaters. These huge vultures are scavengers that feed on 'carrion' (meat from dead animals). Vultures often pick at the bones left behind by predators like cheetahs and lions.

What on Earth?

Big rhea!

The greater rhea is a huge bird. It can grow to the amazing height of 1.5 metres (five feet) - that is higher than most cars !

Many birds use grasses to build nests in the scattered trees or shrubs. Others nest in holes in the ground, or hide in long grasses.

Vultures

What **insects** live in the grasslands?

Grasslands are alive with thousands of insects like bees and butterflies. They drink the sweet nectar from flowers. As they feed, pollen lands on them and they carry it from one flower to another. This fertilises the flowers making them produce seeds and berries. But insects aren't all good. In temperate zones, insects and worms can eat more grass than any other creatures!

Termite mound

skyscrapers?

This huge mound of earth is a termite city. These mounds can be six metres (20 feet) tall! Inside millions of termites live and work in a maze of rooms, tunnels and ventilation holes. The Queen termite lays about 20,000 eggs each day which are cared for by worker termites.

What do butterflies drink?

Regal fritillary butterfly

This very rare butterfly lives on the North American prairies, meadows and marshes. It drinks the nectar of flowers like red clover, milkweed and mountain mint.

Invasion!

A locust swarm looks like a vast swirling black cloud. There can be more than **Fifty billion locusts** in a swarm!!!!

chomp chOmp!

What are locusts?

Locusts

Locusts are a kind of large, leaf-eating grasshopper. In times of drought they swarm together in tall columns which can be as tall as 1.6 kilometres (one mile)! Then they swoop down and eat every plant in sight.

Why are grasslands important?

There are at least 7,500 different grass plants. Grasses like wheat, oats, corn, barley and rice have been a vital source of food for thousands of years. Exotic grassland flowers grow in our parks and gardens and are used in some medicines too. Farming has reduced natural grasslands and some of its original plants have been lost.

What can you make with grass?

Building bricks can be made by mixing grasses with earth and dung. Grass can also be used as roof thatch.

What can happen if grassland is ploughed?

Cereals are now grown on ancient North American prairies. These crops do not have deep natural roots like grass which holds the soil in place. In the 1930s, a drought turned the loose soil into a vast dustbowl. Huge clouds of dust blew for hundreds of kilometres. It affected over 97 million acres of land across five states. Crops failed and thousands of small-time farmers were ruined.

What on Earth?

Hot Earth

Grassland roots hold masses of moisture. They also provide much of the world's oxygen. They help to keep the Earth cool - as their roots absorb harmful gases that can lead to global warming.

Are grasslands under threat?

Nearly three quarters of the world's food is grown in grassland areas, yet only two percent of original grasslands remain. Many of its plants and creatures are now under threat. When a natural grassland area is cleared for other use, many species are lost too.

In North America, thousands of rattlesnakes are killed each year with chemicals that are harmful to wildlife habitats and water systems.

Where is the world's biggest seedbank?

In 1975 The Fermi National Acceleration Laboratory in Chicago created its own grassland habitat as part of a conservation project. In Ethiopia in Africa, the world's biggest grass seed bank preserves grass species.

How would you survive in grasslands?

We grow wheat, maize and barley on grassland, to make anything from cornflakes to bread. But be careful - some grasslands are home to tigers, leopards, lions and they would love to have you for lunch!

Grassland Dangers

Lion If a lion attacks you make a lot of noise and try to scare it away.

Rattlesnake If you are bitten by a rattlesnake - keep the wound below heart level. Call emergency services on your two-way radio.

Malaria This disease kills over a million people a year and is transmitted by mosquitoes. Sleep under a mosquito net and wear some repellent.

What to take Check-list

Be sure to wear **long trousers** in case a snake bites your ankle. Carry a long **knife** to hack your way through tall grasses. Be sure to take a **compass**, the biggest grassland in Russia stretches over 2,500 miles. Take a good pair of **boots** for walking and a **box of matches** to light a fire at night to keep warm. Take an **alarm** to scare off attacking animals and be certain to take a **two-way radio** to call for help. Remember **traps** to catch your dinner and enough fresh **water** for the journey.

Grassland facts

Blue gentian flowers grow in temperate grasslands across the world. Their roots have been used to cure stomach ache!

The burrows of a prairie dog town have been known to stretch for 116,549 square kilometres (45,000 square miles) underground.

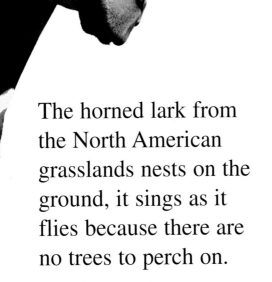

Giraffe

The horned lark from the North American grasslands nests on the ground, it sings as it flies because there are no trees to perch on.

There are 100 types of grasshopper on the American prairies! Some only eat flowers and clear the soil for grass to grow. But farmers think they are a pest.

Tropical grasses can grow 2.2 centimetres (1 inch) in just one day when heavy rains fall.

Some termites make their own food! They grow vegetable moulds and then eat them.

The female elephant has the longest pregnancy of any mammal - 20 to 21 months.

The giant anteater has a long sticky tongue. Its tongue measures about 60 centimetres (24 inches) in length.

The Queen termite is up to 100 times bigger than the workers.

Glossary

Bacteria Tiny living animals.

Burrow A hole or tunnel dug by a small animal.

Camouflage Patterns and colours that help a plant or creature to hide in its habitat.

Continent An individual land mass (like Australia).

Dry temperate A climate that has cold winters and hot summers.

Fungus Spongy vegetable growth, like a mushroom.

Global warming A rise in the earth's temperature.

Habitat The natural environment of a plant or animal.

Herbivores Plant-eating mammals.

Hot tropical A climate that is always hot through its dry season and wet season.

Migrate To move on from one place to another.

Pampas The South American name for tall, swaying grasslands.

Plateaux Areas of high flat ground.

Protozoa Tiny living animals.

Species A group of plants or creatures with similar features and habits.

Ostrich

What do you **know** about the grasslands?

1 What are tall swaying grasses called?

2 How fast can the greater rhea bird run?

3 Why is the baobab tree so useful?

4 What is the Russian word for grasslands?

5 Whose home does the black-footed ferret steal?

6 Which creature builds a mound with air vents?

7 How many stomachs do bison and cattle need to digest grass?

8 How can animal droppings be useful?

9 Do fires kill off grasslands?

10 What do vultures feed on?

Can you guess how much a rhinoceros weighs?

Go to page 32 for the answer!

Index

Pictures are shown in **bold.**

Answers

1 Pampas. (See page 9)
2 They can run at 64 kilometres (40 miles) per hour. (See page 20)
3 Its hollow trunk holds water. (See page 17)
4 Steppe. (See page 9)
5 The black-footed ferret steals the prairie dog's home. (See page 15)
6 The termite builds a home with air vents. (See page 22)
7 Bison and cattle have four stomachs to digest grass. (See page 18)
8 Seeds are shed in their droppings. (See page 18)
9 No, the grasslands quickly recover. (See page 13)
10 Carrion, meat from dead animals. (See page 21)

An adult rhinoceros weighs about **five tonnes.** That's the weight of three and a half family cars.